Food for Thought

Teresa Towell

At the Cross Publishing

At the Cross

Paragould, AR 72450

Ttowell7@gmail.com

Published by At the Cross Publishing

ISBN-13:978-0692958315
ISBN-10:0692958312

Scriptures taken from the King James Version. Copyright 2007

By Thomas Nelson, Inc. All rights reserved.

Acknowledgements

Thank you, Lord for the Inspiration to write these articles.

The Articles in "Food for Thought" were published

By the Paragould Daily Press;

From: years 2016-2017

Index

The Word Does Not Go Out Void

Have you ever felt as though there was something more that you needed to be doing for God? Have you tried to make excuses and tell yourself, well I am not a preacher or teacher, so what I say is not important. Maybe you have even said to yourself "why would anyone want to listen to me". Do not let Satan have the victory over you and steal the blessings that God has for you. In each and every area in one's life or situation there is work to be done. I have been preaching and teaching for several years and from my own personal experience, a vast majority of doing a work for God may be accomplished in a break room, on the job, or at a luncheon. Have you stopped today and spoke to someone about the Lord? Have you told of the "miracle "that you received because you are able to get out of bed and go to your job? If this is the case, then you have had the opportunity to be a witness for our Heavenly Father.

One may not feel that his or her own personal experiences are important, but when you tell your story to an individual that may not realize or have yet become aware of God's goodness, the word of God becomes alive and through his spirit, the words you speak may enter into the heart of unbelief. In the book of Isaiah, the word states "so shall my word be that goeth forth out of my mouth: it shall not return unto me void, but it shall accomplish that which I please, and it shall prosper in the thing whereto I sent it" (CH, 55:11).

1

I have stood before many crowds in service and when the message was finished, I ask myself did anyone hear anything that was spoken in the room tonight. I remember praying and asking the Lord to show me the fruit of my labor. I have come in contact with hundreds, maybe even thousands of people while in this ministry and for a long period of time I would meet people in service and may not see them again for months or years. One day while I was visiting another town, I saw a young lady, she appeared to be trying to get my attention from across the store parking lot; the young lady ran to me and hugged me, in my surprise, I hugged her back. The young lady asks, "you don't remember me do you", I did not remember. The young lady spoke of hearing a message that I had preached and how the Lord, through my words had changed her life. Finally, I knew someone had heard the words that the Lord had given me. Another instance, I had taken a patient to the doctor's office, while sitting quietly with a patient, the Lord spoke to me and told me to go and talk with a woman that was sitting in the waiting area. Reasoning within myself I felt that this woman was going to think that I was crazy. I have never seen this woman before. The Lord told me to tell this woman that he loved her and that she was not alone, that he wanted to help her through her tough times. I walked over to the woman and proceeded to greet her, I then told the woman the words that the Lord had given me. The woman just looked at me, she said a few words and left.

Years later, I was in a store a woman approached me, she looked as though she had seen a ghost. The woman said, "you came to me one day in a doctor's office, and you told me that the Lord loved me and that he wanted to help me". The woman said I hadn't accepted the Lord as my savior then, I had been going through a rough time with my husband and my health. She proceeded to say "but after you came to me that day, I gave my life to the Lord, I am going to church, and I am happier now than I have ever been. Through one simple act of obedience, a life was changed. Will you be willing to hear and obey?

Do not be afraid to speak to your neighbor, your coworker or friend about the Lord, the word will be heard. It is wonderful to have men and women of God to minister the word in congregations, on the television and radio, but he is also in the factories, the offices, and in the grocery stores. Do not be afraid to let your voice be heard, let the spirit lead and guide you.

Let Your Light Shine

The Apostle Paul tells us to "walk worthy of the vocation wherewith ye are called" (Ephesians 4:1,). To walk worthy, what does it mean to walk worthy? One might say that you should love the Lord, love your neighbors, and follows the commandments, what more can one do? First, we know that one must be saved. After giving one's life to the Lord and accepting him one must walk the "daily walk". Living for him is more than attending church, and reading our bibles. One must follow the plan of salvation, become Christ like, and lay oneself aside to help others.

One day while working a coworker came to me asking "I help when I can, and I don't do anything bad, will I make it in to Heaven? Obviously, that is a judgment call and one an individual cannot make. However, because she asked it opened the door that I might instruct her on how to be saved. Instruction does not come from opinions, it comes from the word of God. We proceeded to talk further and discussed the plan of salvation. In the book of Acts, the bible tells us to "Repent and be baptized in the name of Jesus Christ and ye shall receive the gift of the Holy Ghost" (Ch. 2:38). There is a plan, we all must follow the plan, good intentions are not enough.

To become Christ like, how do you present yourself in the most difficult situations? Do you remain faithful? The cares of this life often bring uncertainty, but you can trust the Lord in your darkest hour. A few examples might include: smile when you don't feel as though you can, encourage your brother or sister even though your prayers have not yet been answered, lend a helping hand when your pressed for time yourself, and pray in the midnight hour even though you must be up at five o'clock in the morning for work.

One must be willing to set their own needs aside and help others that may be less fortunate. In Mark, a young man came to Jesus and asked, "good master, what shall I do that I may inherit eternal life"? Jesus answered him and said 'Thou knowest the commandments". (Ch. 10:19). I imagine the young man felt confused, he proceeded to say that he has done these things since he was young. Then Jesus said go and sell what thou have and give to the poor. The Bible states that the man had great wealth, the man was saddened by what the Lord had told him to do (Ch.10: 20-22). So, do these scriptures tell me that money and the things of this world was more important to him than the Lord? What is important to you today? Do you want others to see Jesus in you, to be an example and walk in all holy manner of conversation? The examples I have given are just a few of many things that one can do to walk Christ like. Receive the Lord, do what you know to do and let the light that shines within you shine for all the world to see.

Trust in the Lord, resist the devil

"I feel so alone, no matter what I do the situation has not changed, things are not getting better", these were the words that I heard her say. Many individuals feel alone and discouraged at some point in time in their lives. Often too many times, one may spend a great deal of time and effort trying to fix situations or circumstance that are virtually impossible to fix. One may try everything else before finally calling on the Lord, which can leave one completely exhausted. Reach out to the Lord, be mindful of the words you speak, and resist the devil.

For every problem that one may face the Lord will have an answer; the trials and the storms of this life may cloud one's judgment, but it is in those times that you need him the most. In Peter the word tells us to" humble ourselves under the mighty hand of God, that he may exalt you in due time. Casting all your care upon him, for he careth for you (Ch. 5:7-8). The answer may not come "right now", but it will come.

Choose carefully what you say, and the words that you speak over your life. Matthew tells us that "By thy words thou shalt be justified and by thy words thou shall be condemned" (Ch. 12:37). You may have never thought that the words you speak affect your life, but clearly the scripture tells us they do. Do you know someone that regardless of what may be going on in their life, there is always something wrong, or at least that is what they will tell you; In my experience, their situation usually does not change. One needs to speak life, not doubt and disbelief. If you are asking God to move, believe that he will.

Finally, be mindful and do not listen to every voice, not every voice that speaks to you comes in the name of the Lord. Every thought that you have is not necessarily true, nor is it reality. You may be thinking "what do you mean voices", when doubt begins to fill your mind and negativity creeps in, that is not from the Lord. For instance, you will not get that promotion, you are not qualified, or you have been living in addiction for years, you will never be set free from those strongholds. In James the Bible says to "Submit yourselves therefore to God, Resist the devil, and he will flee from you" (Ch. 4:7). Take a stand, know that negative thinking is not from God. Believe that he is working in your situation even though you have not seen the manifestation. If you find yourself in need today, whether it is financially, spiritually, physically, socially or emotionally, call upon him, he is more than able to provide. There is not a situation or circumstance that he does not already know about, he is waiting on you.

A time to be thankful and help one another

In Ecclesiastes, the scripture tells us "to everything there is a season, and a time to every purpose under the Heaven" (Ch. 3:1), November is a time of celebration and of giving thanks. Many individuals will take time to remember what they have been thankful for throughout the year. Family, friends, coworkers, even strangers will reach out to one another. Let us be thankful, reach out to those in need, and remember the real reason for our celebration.

To be thankful, what does it mean to be thankful? To be glad that something is happening, to be accepting of someone or pleased with one's situation? There are many situations that one can find themselves in daily that can be gratifying, let us not take for granted the little things in our lives. Recently I spoke with a young woman about how so many times we take for granted those "little" things. This young lady reminded me of a time that our family was without power, many of us can remember the great "ice storm", when we struggled to stay warm. To my family this was definitely not a small thing. This woman spoke of the ways that her family had managed to have heat and water and how she was so pleased (thankful) when the power was back on. Often too many times we do not think about how much we appreciate something until it is gone.

Many individuals will be spending time over the next few days with family and friends. Some will shop, some will eat more than they should, some will be preparing for the upcoming holidays. However, there are some that may be alone, that may not have the money to purchase items needed for daily meals. Let us be willing to reach out and help those in need, not only during the holiday seasons, but each day. In 1 John, the scripture states "but whoso may have the world's good, and seeth his brother have need, and shutteth up his bowels of compassion from him, how dwelleth the love of God in him" (Ch. 3:17). So, if we see our brother or sisters in need and we turn away and choose not to help them, how can we truly say the love of God is in us?

Finally, and most importantly, let us remember the reason that we can give thanks each and every day, his name is Jesus. In John, scripture states that "All things that were made by him, and without him was not anything made that has been made" (Ch. 1:3). One cannot walk, talk, or even breathe the air that we breathe without him. He not only reaches out in our time of need, he is there through every day. Enjoy your time with family and friends and take time to thank him for all that he has given you.

Walk by Faith and be Blessed

Walk by faith, what is Faith? Hebrews states that "now faith is the substance of things hoped for, the evidence of things not yet seen (Ch. 11:1). What do you hope for? Is the faith that you have right now "enough"? Do you want your prayers answered? Do you want to see your situations change and the Lord work in your life? One needs to walk by faith, let the world see your works, and wait for the manifestation of the Lord.

To walk by faith can be challenging, stepping out in a time of desperation or despair can be scary. To place one's feet on what could possibly be unstable ground is a place some individuals do not want to be. It is easy to walk when you are walking on solid ground, but when you must move and there is nothing there, it is far more difficult. One does not simply live for God by feeling, you must remember what he has already done and seek him expecting. In Hebrews, the Bible says "for he that cometh to God must believe that he is, and that he is a rewarder of those that diligently seek him (Ch. 11:6). Believe that he "is", and he will help you in your time of need.

Let thy works be seen; in James, the Bible states "shew me thy faith without thy works, and I will shew thee my faith by my works" (Ch. 2:18). To see the Lord move, one must first take a step. For example, when my children were small there was a time that we needed food. There were only a few canned goods in the cabinets and the refrigerator was bare; I remember thinking "Lord what am I going to do". I remembered a story from the Bible where Jesus fed a multitude with two fish and five loaves of bread (Luke Ch. 9:16). I cleaned out the refrigerator and prayed a simple prayer; "Lord I have cleaned this out, I need you to supply my family with food". Unexpectedly, I received a check in the mail that I had no idea was coming. I was so excited; the Lord saw my faith. The Lord showed up when I was at a loss. I sought him, I stepped out by faith, and the rewards came.

Wait, no one wants to hear wait. Would you not prefer a "yes" or "no"? The Lord does not always give an answer quite that simple, oftentimes he simply says wait. The manifestation of your prayers and works will come if you believe. You may not know how, you may not when, but if you stand fast he will make a way. Let the Lord show you how good he can be. You may be looking for a fire in the sky, but he may answer in the still small voice.

Pray and see your prayers answered

Lord I need this, Lord I want this, Lord can you do this for me? Does this sound familiar? The Lord wants us to lean on him, he wants us to depend on him, we are his children; However, we must desire a personal relationship with the Lord not only in our time of need and want, but every day. In prayer, thank him for what you already have, ask for what you need and put him first and above everything else.

There are many ways to pray, each one may pray differently; however, I believe we must first get his attention, for example call him by name, e.g., heavenly father, Lord, then start with a prayer of thanks. We recently celebrated Thanksgiving, and for the most of us we took time to remember why we are thankful and for what, however we should think on these things daily. One day I heard a young woman speaking and she asked a question, "what if you only had today what you thanked the Lord for yesterday? What would you have?

Another step, we need to ask, in Matthew the scripture states to "ask, and it shall be given you; seek and ye shall find; knock, and it shall be opened unto you:" (Ch. 7:7). The Lord already knows what you have need of and the desires of your heart. As an act of obedience if one will ask you shall receive. There is nothing that you have need of that the Lord does not have the power and ability to provide. As with any relationship, a key component is communication, the Lord wants to hear from you.

Put the Lord first and above all things. Put him first, what do you mean put him first? The Bible states that our God is a jealous God (Exodus 34:14). One does not need to let anything become more important in their life that him. Anything can be more important, things one may not have ever considered. An individual, a hobby, even social media could become your "idol". An individual, yes, an individual, one can become completely wrapped up in a person to a point that they have lost sight of their relationship with the Lord. Social media, do you spend more time on social media than you may praying, fasting, or seeking his face? Gaming, do you spend time on the Xbox? Do you spend so much time trying to reach that next level that suddenly you think I will pray and read my Bible tomorrow? Do not allow anything to hinder your walk with God. A relationship with the Lord is not only on Sunday, but seven days a week.

Finally, thank him for what he has already done and given you, ask him when you are in need, and seek that personal relationship with him and you will be blessed.

A time to celebrate our Savior

As a child growing up I remember the anticipation of the holidays as they approached, the cakes made with cocoa, the smell of turkey baking in the oven, the silver Christmas tree that my mother put up so carefully. Most importantly, I remember celebrating the birth of our Savior, Jesus Christ. Christmas time is a time to celebrate with family and friends and rejoice over the birth of our savior.

A celebration, what does it mean to celebrate? A time of rejoicing, having a party, being thankful for someone or something? A celebration for one may take days, weeks, possibly months to plan; one must decorate, prepare the menu and then there is the guest list. Everything must be perfect, right? Why not celebrate in style? However, Christmas is about celebrating the birth of our savior. Christmas has become so commercial, that it seems for some that the true meaning is lost. Celebrating Christmas is not about the most expensive gift or spending so much money that you are trying to pay it back for a year. I recently spoke with a young lady, and she told me that Christmas has gotten so busy that she dreads to see this time of year come.

As you gather around the tree to open your Christmas gifts or meet with your family and friends, let us remember the reason for the season; In Mark, scripture states that an angel of the Lord appeared unto Mary "and the angel said unto her, fear not, Mary: for thou hast found favor with God. And behold thalt shalt conceive in thy womb, and bring forth a son, and shall call his name Jesus. "and that he shall reign over the house of Jacob forever, and of his kingdom there shall be no end (Ch. 16,31-3). Let us not get so busy that we forget the real reason that we celebrate. Let us rejoice over his birth.

Take care of the Physical and Spiritual Body

It's that time again, a time of setting goals and New Year's resolution. For some it may be to spend less and to get your finances in order, for others it might be to lose weight, exercise, and eat better. These things are important in the carnal but let us not forget the spiritual. In this new year, let us work toward not only taking care of the physical, but the spiritual body.

I believe that we need to take care of our physical bodies, in I Corinthians the scripture states "know ye not that ye are the temple of God, and that the spirit of God dwelleth in you? (Ch. 3:16) I have been told since I was a child that one needs to try to eat balanced meals, exercise, and get plenty of rest. However, if one sets goals that are extreme, then one can begin to feel overwhelmed if the weight is not coming off quick enough or progress is slow. Start with the small steps and set goals that are within reach.

To take care of the spiritual body, one may choose to pray more often, read the Bible, and attend church services regularly. These things are important to maintain a personal relationship with the Lord and find strength. In Hebrews, the scripture states 'but to do good and communicate forget not, for with such sacrifices God is well pleased" (Ch. 13:16). Do you want that personal relationship and to grow in him? If so, then you must plan to give him your time also.

Again, set not a goal that is "out of reach". Don't simply say I am going to read three chapters in the Bible so it can be marked done, read five verses and study them. Set a time to pray and if something hinders, pray later. Always remember if you fall short of your goals, you can start again. Find a balance, plan to take care of the physical and the spiritual body.

Study and Prepare Yourself

In the world we live in today, the advancement of technology has made some things so easy, one can simply "google" anything and find a quick answer. However, easy may not always be the best method. Let us study and prepare ourselves that we know the word and can relay it to others.

In 2 Timothy, Paul states that one should "study to shew thyself approved unto God, . . . (Ch 2:15). How does one study that they may be approved? There are many things that one can do, for example: prepare thyself that when called upon or the opportunity arises, you will know what to do and how to help others.

Study and search out the scriptures; the word of God was not meant to be read like a magazine; Yes, many read it that way, however, if one hurries through the word and does not take the time to search out the meaning, you may not remember it later. Many have said "I do not understand the word or the meaning of it". If one truly seeks the Lord for the understanding the spirit will bring intersession and give you what you need.

Be prepared, if one finds themselves in a situation and is asked about certain things, be ready to give an answer. It is possible that the question may be asked "what does the bible say I must do to be saved", would you know the answer? Would you know what to say if one asks about healing? If we study the scripture and hide his word in our heart, then we can tell others what to do or where it can be found in the word of God. We will all be held accountable. Whether you are a minister, a bus driver, or a grocery clerk and you received the Lord as your personal savior, there will always be an opportunity to witness.

Treasures in Heaven

The American dream- Marriage, children, a good job, a house with the two-car garage and the family pet. These things are all blessings, we must have money to provide for our needs, we must be able to work to pay for food and shelter, but let us not forget to work toward our treasures that will be in Heaven.

As a child growing up my family was poor; my daddy worked in the factory long hours to provide for our needs. I have several siblings and often things were scarce; life was hard, and we did not have the finer things, but we had love. My daddy is a man who believes in Christ, so we went to church "a lot". We were taught to appreciate what we have and not worry so much about what we have here, but rather what we will have in Heaven.

Sunday school was a favorite time, a valuable lesson I learned in my early years is found in Matthew, scripture states "Lay not up for yourselves treasure upon earth, where most and rust doth corrupt, and where thieves break through and steal: but lay up for yourselves treasure in Heaven, where moth nor dust doth corrupt, and where thieves do not break through nor steal: for where your treasure is there your heart will be also" (Ch. 6: 19-21).

How does one store up "treasures in heaven"? Have you ever had a sudden urge, or the spirit rises in you to say something even though you had no idea? When the lord speaks through you and someone feels led to receive him, you may have earned a star in your crown.

My grandmother sang a song "Sending up Timbers", timbers were to build her mansion; not a mansion of wood, but in Heaven. My grandmother's prayers were the timbers, and she prayed many nights for her children and grandchildren; She used her energy to pray for those she loved, she stored up her treasures in Heaven. Will you place your hope in things on this earth that will decay, or will you plan for those things that will bring life everlasting?

Revelation paints a picture of what Heaven will be like, "streets made of gold, walls made of Jasper, and gates made with pearl (Ch. 21: 19-21). I am not sure that one could even begin to grasp how beautiful it will be, but there is nothing in this life that can compare to what the Bible states it shall be like. Where will store your treasures?

His grace is more than enough

Have you ever felt like a failure? Have you felt that no matter what you do that it is not enough? No matter how hard you try do "what is right" you cannot seem to get there? Everyone makes mistakes, and everyone fails, you do not have to earn his grace, look to him and he will lift you up.

Oftentimes, in living the Christian walk one may struggle to be what God wants them to be. One might say, I want to walk in his ways and his will, I want to grow stronger in him, but it is so hard; you are not alone. I have been teaching for many years and I have never met anyone that does not struggle at some point in time in their life. There are good days but there will also be hard days; If you feel that you are not enough, that is because by yourself, you are not, let us remember, "he is". Scripture states "my grace is sufficient for thee: for my strength is made perfect in weakness. Most gladly therefore will I rather glory in my infirmities, that the power of Christ may rest upon me" (II Corinthians, 12:9). Even though it is hard, through is grace one can find rest.

In Peter the scripture states "I stir up your pure minds by way of remembrance" (Ch. 3:1), the Lord takes my mind to a place in my early years as a Christian, when I would make a mistake or fail I thought that there was something that I needed to do or could do to earn his grace; I thought that long prayers or reading many chapters in the Bible would make up for the

23

mistakes that I had made. It was not until one day while reading the word, the Lord spoke to me (as if he was speaking in an audible voice) "my daughter, there is nothing you need to do, simply ask for forgiveness, my grace is enough. I was absolutely "wowed" at that moment; All I need to do is simply ask the Lord to forgive me and help me, I did not have to do anything to earn his grace or love.

Finally, know that life can be hard, situations can be tough, and not a one of us can do anything without his help. You cannot earn grace, simply pray and receive it with gladness.

Christians need to pull together and pray for one Another

Turn on the television, the radio, or open the news on the internet, what do you see or hear? Do you hear of murder, violence, drug use and abuse? Yes, one can hear of all these things mentioned in one setting, rarely does anyone broadcast about the good that has happened. However, good things do happen daily. "Now" is a time to pull together, pray for this nation and our leaders, and know that God is still working for his children.

Individuals that love the Lord gather daily and weekly in churches, homes, and even in parking lots to speak of the Lord and his goodness. Why do they continue to gather and lift one another up? Why do they continue even though the wickedness of the world continues? Though Satan continues to paint the picture that bad news is all there is, the church, (his people) knows that there is so much more. There are still people that believe and trust in God. There are still parents that teach their children right from wrong. There are individuals continually striving to make it to Heaven.

The word instructs us to pray for our leaders, in 1 Timothy scripture states "I exhort therefore, that first of all, supplications, prayers, intercessions, and giving of thanks, be made for all men; For kings, and for all that are in authority; that we may lead a peaceable life in all goodliness and honesty (Ch 2:3). There appears to be constant confusion upon this land, but as Christians if we will pray and bind together, the word states that "if my people which are called by my name, will humble themselves and pray and seek my face and turn form their wicked ways; then will I hear from heaven and will forgive their sin and heal their land (2 Chronicles, CH. 7 :14). A few years back, I remember a time when gas prices were soaring, suddenly the talk of praying for gas prices to go down was discussed at work, church, in the grocery store, in the salons etc. A need arose, people prayed, and gas prices begin to fall and continue to remain down.

He hears the prayers of his people. Let us bind together and pray for our country and leaders, speak positive, and dwell on the good. Yes, you will hear bad news and it may appear as though evil is all around, but the Lord is forever in control of all situations.

A Solid Foundation

Have you heard it said, that before you can build a house you must first lay the foundation? In I Corinthians, the body is referred to as the temple of God (Ch. 3: 16), and how one chooses to live their life will determine how the foundation is built. One can choose to walk in the ways of this world, or build upon the rock. In Psalms, the scripture states that "the Lord is the Rock" (Ch. 18: 2). One must believe that he is, receive him as your personal savior, and build upon a solid foundation.

In Hebrews, the Bible says "for he that cometh to God must believe that he is and that he is a rewarder of those that diligently seek him (Ch. 11:6), One might ask, how do you believe in something you cannot see? Jesus told Thomas, "because thou have seen me, thou hast believed: blessed are they who have not seen and have believed" (John, 20:29). Often too many times we begin to doubt due to uncertainty, one cannot see the Lord, yet that does not mean that he does not exist. It is possible to know that he is with you because he will speak to your heart and you can feel his presence. A simple analogy: I find myself thinking of the wind, one cannot see the wind, but as it blows you can feel and hear it. When the Lord speaks to your heart you may not see him, but you know and can feel his presence. If the Lord has truly spoken to your heart, you will know, and you must believe that he is speaking.

One must not only believe that he is but also receive him. Receive him, what do you mean receive him? the Apostle Paul wrote "that if thou shalt confess with thy mouth the Lord Jesus, and believe in thy heart that God hath raised him from the dead, thou shalt be saved (Romans 10: 9). You must receive him into your heart and ask him to forgive you for the sins that you have committed. Jesus is a gentleman, you must invite him in.

Do not be led by feelings, let the Lord lead you

Fear- a common feeling or emotion among many individuals, However, that is exactly what it is "a feeling". Individuals experience good feelings and bad feelings, examples might include: excitement, joy, distress, discouragement, etc. One can experience many of these feelings in only a short time. One should search for the truth and not allow "any" feelings to lead and guide you.

Where does one look to find the truth? How does one know that which will be? The truth can be found in his word. In Isaiah, the scripture states" the grass whithereth, the flower fadeth: but the word of our God shall stand for ever (Ch: 40:8). The Lord has provided us with exactly what we need and that is his "Word". No matter what you are feeling, one can find an answer if you look to him.

You might be thinking, look to him? There are many ways the Lord provides guidance; I have seen the Lord answer by speaking scripture when one is need, sending an individual to speak to you at just the right time, or by simply speaking in a still small voice. He will send an answer if you earnestly search. For example, recently I had been really studying and reading in his word, I was searching for an understanding of word that that the Lord had spoke to me (the Lord often speaks in parables, and I did not understand the word he had given) I continued to read and "suddenly" I had the answer that I had been searching for. I was so excited, I did not need anyone to tell me I knew he was speaking. I made an effort and he sent the answer.

Finally, let him lead and guide you down the right path and do not be led by feelings of anxiety, fear, doubt or disbelief.

Pray for peace for your children

The fall season brings cooler weather, the turning of leaves, bonfires, and for a majority of families, children returning to school. Returning to school can be exciting and a little scary for some. As a parent, you can lead and guide your children through this time. Let us pray over our children daily for peace and protection.

As a young child, I remember the anticipation of the first day, the excitement of riding the school bus, making new friends, and getting new books. However, I also felt a fear of the unknown. Regardless of a child's age, there are times that they will experience fear. When one takes the time, and prays over their child, this can bring not only moments of teaching, but through the Lord's spirit, it can bring peace. In Philippians scripture states" and the peace of God, which passeth all understanding shall keep your hearts and minds" (Ch. 4:17).

Recently in teaching my Sunday school class, I discussed going back to school, as we talked I realized that most of my children had a fear of not meeting any new friends. I prayed for my students and explained to them that God can send them friends (as some were new at their schools). They actively listened, and I could see a calming and peace in their faces.

As a parent, you may also struggle with fear, I have had many conversations with mothers or fathers that were worried about the safety of their child or their child meeting a bully. My response to them most often will be "I cannot always go with my children, but my heavenly father can". I have stopped my children before they walked out the door, took them by the hand, and prayed for peace and the Lord's protection over them. In Psalms, the scripture states "For he shall give his angels charge over thee, to keep thee in all thy ways" (91:11). Know that the Lord will send angels to encamp about them and when you cannot be with them, he can.

Speak the Word

Are you searching for an answer? Have you asked the Lord to lead and guide you? Do you need to make a decision, but you become fearful that you will make the wrong one? Many individuals struggle with these questions- listen to the Lord, stand still, and receive an answer.

A question repeatedly asked me over the years, "how do you know you hear from the Lord"? As a young Christian I felt confused and did not understand about the Lord's voice. I had heard preachers, teachers, and elders of the church, speak about the Lord "speaking to them". I prayed, yet I still heard nothing. Why haven't I heard? I remembered rationalizing within myself, Lord, I walk in your ways, then, the Lord gave me a scripture: In John, the scripture states " my sheep hear my voice, and I know them, and they know me" (CH: 10:27). After praying for what felt to be a lengthy period, I begin to hear. I will never forget the first time that I realized that the Lord had spoke to me, I had a "wow" moment. I was traveling down the road in my car, looking out across the fields, he began to talk to me, I knew. I then realized, that was not the first time that he had spoken to me but now, "I knew".

Stand still, what do you mean stand still? There are seasons in everyone's life that one can do nothing to change or "fix". However, waiting on an answer can be difficult. Many individuals seek the Lord, ask, pray, and expect an answer, and they expect that answer "now". Unfortunately, answers do not always come now. In Isaiah, the scripture states, "but they that wait upon the Lord shall renew their strength; they shall mount up with wings as eagles; they shall run, and not be weary; they shall walk and not faint" (Ch: 40:31).

Are you searching for your answer or an answer from the Lord? I remember praying about a situation and the Lord said an answer will come. I continued to search and found myself getting ahead of the Lord; The Lord moved on my request, I received what I had asked for and I was miserable. I shortly received an answer from the Lord; the answer came easy, transitions were smooth and there was no grief.

In Conclusion, the Lord will send an answer if you ask, seek him with your whole heart, and don't get in a hurry. Granted, some answers will come quicker than others, but it shall be worth the wait.

www.ingramcontent.com/pod-product-compliance
Lightning Source LLC
Chambersburg PA
CBHW040346060426

42445CB00029B/12